OTHER CHILDREN'S BOOKS BY ANDREW SHAFFER

Cryptid Holiday Classics

Mothman's Merry Cryptid Christmas
Mothman's Happy Cryptid Halloween
Mothman's Very Cryptid Valentine's

THE SECRET PET

words and illustrations by
ANDREW SHAFFER

8TH CIRCLE PRESS • LOUISVILLE, KY

dedicated to t.s., my secret pet — a.s.

originally published in french as *L'animal de Compagnie Secret.*

paperback isbn: 9781949769647
hardcover isbn: 9781949769630

also available as an ebook

THE SECRET PET

Etienne has a secret pet that no one else can see.

Etienne has a secret pet he feeds and feeds and feeds.

La Crêperie

Etienne has a secret pet he swims with at the pool.

Etienne has a secret pet he bikes with down *la rue.*

Etienne has a secret pet he plays with in the park.

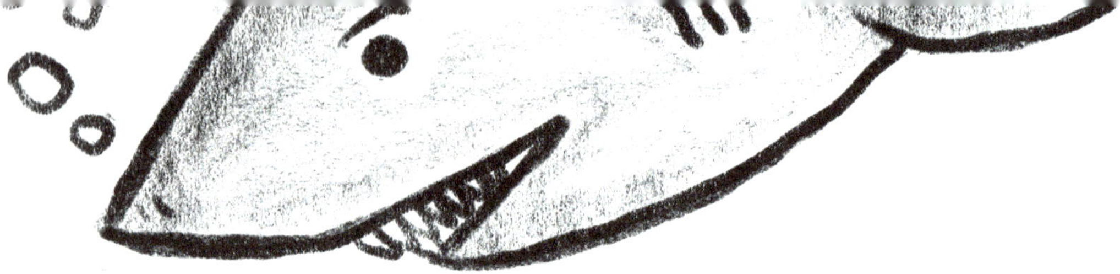

Etienne has a secret pet he takes to see the sharks.

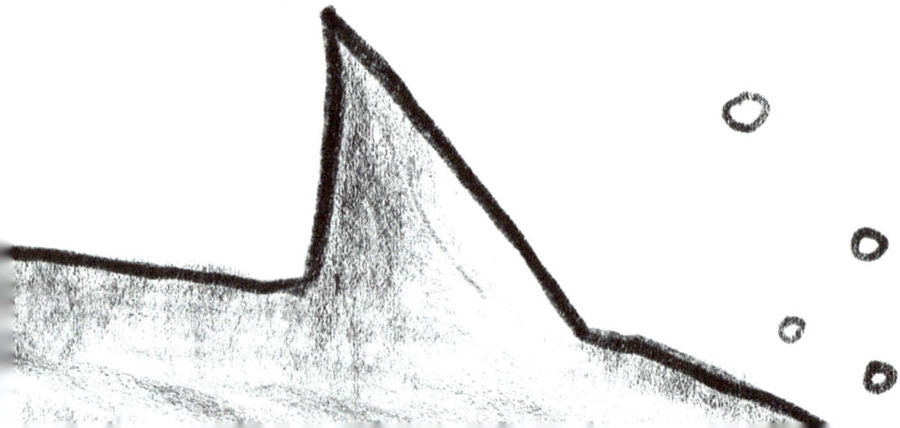

Etienne has a secret pet he reads to every day.

Etienne has a secret pet he drinks with in cafés.

ABSINTHE
DUCROS fils

Etienne has a secret pet he takes to see the sights.

Etienne has a secret pet he sleeps with every night.

Etienne has a secret pet

that makes him

very sick.

Etienne has a secret pet that's long and flat and limp.

Etienne has a secret pet . . .

. . . a tapeworm called Lenore.

Etienne has a secret pet that is secret no more.

FIN.

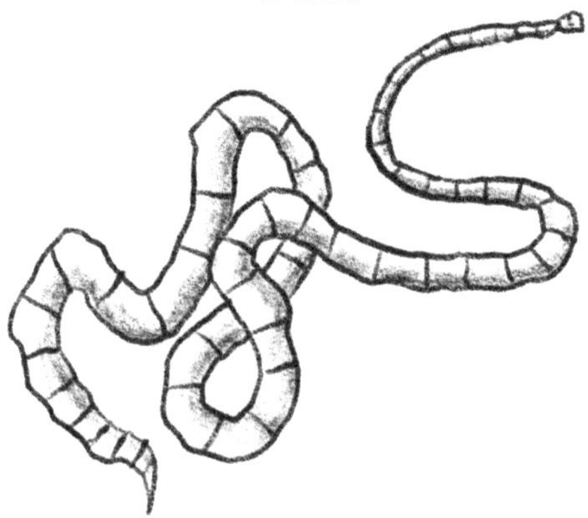

Milton Keynes UK
Ingram Content Group UK Ltd.
UKHW022009110324
439294UK00005B/60

9 781949 769647